# A Celebration of Life Planner

# A Celebration of Life Planner:

## Making Your Memories Your Legacy

Felicia M. Barlow Clar

Visit our website at www.celebratingthedash.com
dba Epilogue Tributes
Barclar Entertainment, LLC
Annapolis, MD 21401
USA

Cover design by Erin Foggoa

ISBN (paperback): 978-1-7368251-2-9
ISBN (PDF): 978-1-7368251-3-6

While the author has made every effort to provide accurate internet addresses at the time of publication, the author does not assume any responsibility for errors or changes that may occur after publication. Further the author and publisher does not have any control over nor assumes any responsibility for third-party websites or their content.

**This workbook is NOT a legal document and does NOT replace the expertise of an attorney, financial advisor, medical practitioner, or others. The author has created a blank workbook for you to use at your own risk, and she has no control over the information you enter. The author and publisher shall in no event be held liable to any party for any direct, indirect, punitive, special, incidental, or other consequential damages arising directly or indirectly from any use of this material, which is provided "as is" and without warranties. The author and publisher assume no liability, responsibility, or damage of any kind as the result of the use or misuse of personal or protected information, such as financial information or other sensitive and/or confidential information you may enter. Please exercise extreme care and protection of this document once you have filled it in.**

*Every man's life ends the same way.*
*It is only the details of how he lived and how he died*
*that distinguish one man from another.*
*~ Ernest Hemingway*

## Namaste

No one will ever exist just like you. You are one of a kind. From your family, to the city you live in, to your talents, hobbies and education, all of these traits and their unique combination belong solely to you. This is precisely why I founded *Epilogue Tributes* and why I created this planner. I saw something missing in the funeral industry — the ability to celebrate the uniqueness that each of us brings to this world.

My deep spiritual beliefs had me questioning why funerals appear so impersonal. Short answer — they are. In the days before the cremation rate rose so dramatically, it made sense to proceed quickly after a death, using templates, and ensuring the burial took place within a week or so. That timeline is no longer a necessity for most.

Not only are there alternatives to a burial, there is a movement towards educating families about their legal rights to care for their own and the many options available to create something uniquely yours.

When my sister died, we did what most families do — we called our funeral home; the one we had just used a year earlier for my beloved stepfather's service. My family came together (again) to plan the details, sitting in their very corporate-like conference room. Everything discussed came from a template or list with some sort of a "pick one of these" option, from the prayer cards to the repast/reception menu (which isn't always available in funeral homes). Even the obituaries the funeral director wrote were akin to a pre-written format with names and adjectives inserted.

The planning experience for both my loved ones was the same: nice, graceful, compassionate. But little presented to us expressed the uniqueness, or legacy, of either of my relatives. We took it upon ourselves to personalize my stepfather's service by wearing his favorite color (red), playing his song (*New York, New York*), inviting our family reverend to perform the service, and serving a special dessert that had symbolic meaning. My stepfather's favorite place was the beach, so that funeral home template worked. Lucky for us, there were also no family squabbles or conflicts.

The problem with planning for my sister was she did not fit *any* template in any way, shape or form. She was a "live by her own rules, unapologetic, life of the party" type with a quick-witted sense of humor that rivaled our greatest comedians. Nothing in the templates and checklist expressed celebration of *her life* to us.

Growing up, I was closest to her, whether as archenemies in grade school or the maid of honor at her wedding. I've been an event and video producer for decades, so thankfully I knew what questions to ask the funeral director in order to work around the templates. Naturally, it was me who was sent home with the checklist to complete the service.

I could hear my sister the entire week that I planned, asking me to tell her life story, not the tragedy of her death. Having a bedroom next to hers all those years had its benefit; I knew what brought her joy. I put together *her* soundtrack and had it playing throughout the building as soon as guests arrived. Our family reverend was asked again to lead the service, knowing he could share personal stories. He and I worked on the program, incorporating significant songs. She loved classic country music's meaningful storytelling, so these were inserted throughout. At the end, I played her favorite Shaggy song that held special significance to her children. Our family had agreed to get up and dance as we knew she would have done. For those who truly understood the moment, they joined in. This created the atmosphere my sister would have loved, and more important, it left people with a sense of joy and gratitude for who she was. One of our friends remarked to me, "If this is appropriate to say…this is the best funeral I've ever been to." That filled my heart for so many reasons.

## Your Celebration of Life Plan

We plan in detail everything from destination weddings to pet birthday parties, but we don't consider one of life's most important transitions until it's staring us in the face… until now.

First, I want you to stop and honor yourself for starting to plan ahead; so few do. Many of us fear talking about mortality for various reasons: "It's too morbid," "It's scary," "It's bad luck," or "I have plenty of time before that happens." The truth is…none of this is true.

The simple facts are: We don't know our fate. Life and death is the very essence of being human. And nobody is going to die simply by talking about it. We also know leaving our loved ones to make final decisions — often, guessing — places enormous stress on them. There is no better way to say "I'm thinking of you and I love you" than with a plan that considers the heavy burden placed on those left behind when loss occurs.

Pre-planning the inevitable is simply *smart.*

Event planning — which is precisely what a Celebration of Life, memorial service or funeral is — has consistently been ranked one of the top five most stressful jobs in North America. Take one look at the television show *Bridezillas* if you need proof about event planning stress. Events have been known to cause meltdowns and drama even amongst the strongest. Now add grief and loss on top of that. This is precisely what the funeral industry has created, albeit not intentionally.

This workbook is intended to help ease the stress and will guide your loved ones on how to truly memorialize a beautiful life. *Yours.*

This planner also provides information an event professional may know, but a funeral director may not…their expertise, after all, is death, grief, and service. As the end-of-life industry expands, the list of alternatives and choices grows. America is a diverse nation, yet that is rarely depicted when you step into a funeral home. Now, you get to reclaim your *entire* life and decide what the word "funeral" or "celebration of life" means, because it's yours. It could be an intimate home gathering, a candlelight vigil held in a meaningful location, or a big bash in a dance hall for all to joyously express gratitude and thank you for being a part of their lives.

Everybody wants to be remembered and to know they mattered to their family, friends, and community. This is where *you* get to have input into those memories.

With the many options you might have never heard of, and certainly more to come, my intention is to lay out many of these for your consideration. You will most likely want your funeral to honor what you stood for. Let your heart and deepest values guide you to create a service that tells *your* story.

You can change your mind at any point, so I suggest using a pencil to complete your planner. It is important that you share with your Executor and/or Designated Agent or a trusted loved one your desire to implement what you have detailed in this planner.

You want to consider budget as a value of yours, however I suggest you not fixate on costs, because prices and services change. Decide first if you want something lavish, simple, or in-between. There is literally something for everyone. An event professional (i.e., Sacred Life Celebrant) can work with your budget and convey your story.

## This is Your Life

The next decision to make is whether you want this to be a Living Tribute to you — where you get to be a guest in celebrating your own legacy and sharing in your loved ones' remarks — or would you prefer a memorial after your death?

- □ Living Tribute
- □ Celebration of Life

It is important to know that your plan may only be an expression of your final wishes, unless it is a Living Tribute where you can participate. You can ask your loved ones to fulfill these wishes to the best of their ability, but there is no guarantee that they will be able to make all details happen. Funds should be considered in your estate plan.

I am very sensitive to the choices made by terminally ill adults, be that choosing medical alternatives or embracing "death with dignity." I believe a Living Tribute is one more compassionate way to offer comfort and peace.

I also suggest naming a "Designated Agent" for fulfilling end-of-life plans. In more than half the states, there is a statutory obligation for survivors to honor the written wishes of the deceased. Find details for your state through the Funeral Consumers Alliance: https://funerals.org/?consumers=legal-right-make-decisions-funeral

## Type of Service

The type of service you desire is mainly limited by your imagination…and perhaps, budget. Your choice may depend on your religious/spiritual beliefs and personal preference.

The most common services are:

- ☐ **Visitation:** A visitation, also known as a "viewing", takes place before or instead of a funeral. People gather to express their sympathies and say their final goodbyes, often in the presence of the body. A viewing can be done publicly or private, and can take place prior to a cremation.

  *Note: Loved ones should be aware embalming is not a requirement in most situations.*

- ☐ **Funeral:** A funeral typically occurs within a week of death. It is a formal ceremony that often includes eulogies, prayers, hymnals, or special readings. It can be religious or secular. A religious ceremony is typically held in a house of worship, while secular ceremonies are more often held at funeral homes.

- ☐ **Graveside Service:** A graveside service typically follows a funeral but can also function as a sole event. It can be limited to family or open to anyone. The service is held at the place of interment, a mausoleum, or a columbarium. If inclement weather is predicted, a tent is often put up to cover a portion of the gathering and grave site.

- ☐ **Home Funeral:** Home funerals are both intimate and affordable. Loved ones can legally prepare the body (but don't have to), acquire the necessary paperwork, hold a vigil or service, and have the body transported to the burial site or crematory (often through a funeral home). This is how death care happened in families until the Civil War. We are seeing a resurgence as advocates help restore the rights of families to perform their own rites, without commercial businesses involved. It can be very healing for those involved.

  *Note: Only 9 states still require a funeral director be hired: Connecticut, Illinois, Indiana, Iowa, Louisiana, Michigan, Nebraska, New Jersey, and New York. For specific State requirements and updates, visit:* https://www.homefuneralalliance.org/state-requirements.html

- ☐ **Cremation Ritual:** Some religions are very specific about the way in which, or if, a cremation should take place, including family participation. You may prefer to have a home funeral or a service held at the crematorium prior to cremation.

- ☐ **Celebration of Life:** This service typically refers to a remembrance taking place after the cremation, meaning there is no body present. It does not need to happen immediately and loved ones should not feel pressure to conform to a schedule. It provides family and friends the opportunity to honor the deceased. Companies such as mine can work with your loved ones to produce your celebration of life, so that you are honored, your details are implemented, and loved ones are given space to grieve.

- ☐ **Living Tribute:** If knowing that death is imminent, or perhaps for those considering medical assistance through Death With Dignity laws, this allows for family and friends to pay respects on a scheduled date. It may lessen the costs and complications of last minute travel and arrangements. Some favor this plan, not from an egotistical need to hear accolades, but for a very kind and considerate reason — to make it easier on loved ones.

- ☐ **Virtual Gathering:** Although offered in some way for years, videoconferencing has risen in popularity since the 2020 pandemic. These are great for immediacy and a way to gather loved ones around the globe, say for a candlelight vigil. However, it is still not as comforting as an in-person gathering, and the technology (and camera angles) needs improvement at many sites. There are event and video professionals that are far better equipped and trained to handle a virtual memorial service than a funeral home.

You can have more than one service to suit your needs, and you are free to choose the pieces that work for you. You can use a funeral home for some needs and a Life Celebrant for others. For example, you can have the traditional visitation prior to the funeral, followed by cremation, and a Celebration of Life at a suitable location at a later date. Or host a home funeral, complemented by a virtual vigil the evening before.

*From the National Home Funeral Alliance:*

"Keeping or bringing a loved one home after death is legal in every state for bathing, dressing, private viewing, and ceremony as the family chooses. Every state recognizes the next-of-kin's custody and control of the body that allows the opportunity to hold a home vigil. Religious observations, family gatherings, memorials, and private events are not under the jurisdiction of the State or professionals in the funeral industry, who have no medico-legal authority unless it is transferred to them when they are paid for service.

No one knows better than the family what's truly necessary or needed when caring for their own after death. When in doubt, know that you already have the most important piece of this puzzle: your own best judgment…and you may now know more than most medical professionals— a funeral home may not be needed at all."

Check your state requirements:
https://www.homefuneralalliance.org/state-requirements.html

## Upfront Decisions and Body Care

You must consider the care and arrangement for your body disposition. This is explained in much more detail in my companion workbook: ***What You Don't Know About End of Life Planning: A guide to discover the death-positive movement, exploring your options, and living and dying with intention.***

Your values may play a considerable role here in regards to religion and environmental impact. Loved ones can find thorough information how to care for your body from the National Home Funeral Alliance. An End-of-Life Doula can also assist.

☐ I prefer my loved ones care for my body at home, if possible.

- Special instructions for the home care and treatment of my body are:

- Personal rituals and/or spiritual practices I'd like incorporated are (include music, colors, flowers, scents, essential oils, crystals, etc.):

☐ I would like an End-of-Life Doula to assist.*

- Name and contact of my preferred End-of-Life Doula:

☐ I prefer (check one): ____burial ____entombment ____green burial

____cremation ____Aquamation ____open-air funeral pyre ____other (specify):

☐ Immediate burial

☐ Direct cremation

☐ I am donating my body or organs to (specify):

☐ I prefer a traditional funeral.

☐ I prefer a personalized Celebration of Life.

☐ I prefer a home funeral.

- My "care community" to assist with my home funeral is/are:

☐ Viewing (check one): ____private ____public

☐ Casket: ____open ____closed

☐ I prefer _____ number of viewings.

☐ My clothing preference is: ____current wardrobe ____new clothing

Specify:

☐ Shroud/wrap preference for a green burial. This can be a blanket or some other material you hold dear (specify):

☐ Glasses (for viewing): ____on ____off

☐ Return glasses to family: ____yes ____no

☐ Jewelry to be worn (specify):

☐ Return jewelry to family: ____yes ____no

☐ Rosary: ____yes ____no

☐ I am aware embalming is not required in most circumstances.

☐ I prefer NOT to be embalmed, if possible.

☐ Preference of casket, if buried (check one): ____wood ____metal ____fiberglass ____biodegradable ____wicker ____nothing fancy ____other (specify):

☐ My loved ones can create a personalized casket.

☐ Casket interior color/material preference:

☐ Veterans' service: ____yes ____no

☐ Flag: ____draped ____folded

- Present flag to:

☐ Pallbearers, if casket chosen:

☐ I have prepaid my cemetery plot, mausoleum or columbarium (circle one).

- Located at:

- Cemetery preference, if not prepaid (availability will need to be researched):

☐ I prefer to be placed in a mausoleum/entombment within the cemetery.

☐ Cemetery preference for green burial: ____wood preserve ____private property ____green cemetery (specify):

☐ Grave/Memorial marker: ____granite ____stone ____metal ____other (specify):

- Grave marker inscription:

☐ Preference of urn*, if cremated (check one): ____wood ____metal ____stone ____artisan piece ____biodegradable ____other (specify):

☐ My loved ones can craft a personalized urn.

☐ My loved ones can incorporate my cremains into: ____jewelry ____artwork ____tattoo ____fireworks ____other (specify):

- Urn pendant inscription:

☐ I prefer my cremains be disposed/scattered in a specific manner/location: ____sea ____coral reef ____underwater garden ____tree roots ____garden ____wood preserve ____space ____fireworks ____compost ____mushrooms ____private property ____aerial ____on cemetery grounds** ____a variety of favorite locations**____other (specify):

***Specify your desired location(s) here. Provide as many details as possible, including country and/or significance, so that your ashes are disposed of as you desire.* ***Legal restrictions may apply.***

If you desire your cremains be scattered outside the United States, please talk to your Executor and/or Designated Agent. Calls should be made to the appropriate Embassy to see if there are any restrictions. Most countries welcome this. ****A TSA approved urn and cremation certificate will be needed.***

☐ Private property for: ____burial ____ash scattering

- Address:

☐ I have researched, city, county, and state regulations for burial/cremains.

☐ I have permission from property owner legally documented.

☐ Name of the property owner granting permission:

- If chosen, I prefer the budget for my casket or urn be: ____ inexpensive ____moderate/middle ____lavish

- I intend expenses for my service to be paid from:

## Organizing My Tribute

Hiring an event strategist (ex. Life Celebrant) will ensure your plans are implemented and logistics run smoothly. These professionals have a wider knowledge of production than a funeral director. They will hire and organize a variety of vendors, work with officiants on timelines, manage logistics and details from beginning to end, speak, and/or make introductions at the service or celebration. They also support family, among other tasks that arise. Some event pros can also ensure videos and montages are personal and created as desired.

You can designate one or more family members or a friend to organize your service, but this takes away from their ability to completely enjoy the service and be fully present with loved ones for support and grief.

- My Sacred Life Celebrant is:

- Company name and contact information:

- My preferred Officiant is:

- Officiant's contact information:

## ***My Tribute. My Story. My Legacy***

End of life celebrations, funerals, and memorials should be meaningful and personal. Many current offerings fall short. They offer templates and checklists that so often do not say anything about the person being memorialized. Envision your day and how you want to be remembered.

Consider family traditions, customs and religious and/or spiritual practices that are important to you. Also consider life accomplishments, hobbies, and contributions that are uniquely your own. Listen to your heart, not cultural expectations. Let go of any perceived obligations or practices you do not really want. This is your final opportunity to express your unique spirit. Laughing and fun is perfectly acceptable if that's who you are. So is a party, if that's what you feel is an expression of you. Ask for input from loved ones if you're feeling humble or need help.

In order to get more fully in the moment, I suggest getting comfortable and allowing yourself to relax and let your mind wander. Reflect on your life, your contributions, your family and friends, cherished moments… and how you would like to see your life story unfold.

**What do you see? How do you see the day organized? Write down what you envision or sketch it:**

Below are prompts to guide you with planning. You do not have to complete each item, but record as many details as possible to assist your loved ones. Budget will be a major consideration; for now, simply get your preferences on paper. An event professional is creative and can assist in finding vendors for every detail.

- I prefer: ____ a wake ____candlelight vigil ____picnic ____church service ____big party ____dancing ____jazz/second line ____Zoomeral℠ ____other (specify):

- I prefer: ____ spiritual ____religious (specify religion):

- Service/gathering: ____public ____private
- My favorite flowers are:

*If you are environmentally conscious and planning a green service, you will want to visit this website before you request flowers:*
https://www.sevenponds.com/after-death/environmental-and-social-impact-of-flowers

- Charitable donations in lieu of flowers: ____yes ____no
- Charitable donations in addition to flowers: ____yes ____no

- Charitable organization(s) I would like supported:

- Display the following at my service (special photos, memorabilia, art, etc.):

- Specify if you want anyone to bring a significant object that connected them to your life:

- I prefer: ____live music ____recorded music
- Genre(s) of music I prefer: ____jazz ____big band ____oldies (50s/60s) ____disco/70s ____80s ____90s ____classic rock ____metal ____current rock ____classic country ____current country ____hip hop ____pop ____other (specify):

- I have set up a playlist online: ____yes ____no
- My playlist is available on this streaming service (ex, Spotify, list title & link):

- Favorite live band/entertainers I'd like to perform:

- Special performance I'd like done at my service (ex. family member sings):

- Live musical instruments preferred (ex., jazz trio, harp, bagpipes, second line):

- The musical playlist should include these favorite songs (include title and artist):

- Online commemoration: ____legacy website ____memorial page with guest book ____Facebook page ____other (specify):

- I have a designated URL for my legacy website (specify name):

- My legacy website is already online: ____yes ____no
- Hosting service for my legacy website (specify):

- I have designated someone in my Facebook settings to change my Facebook page to a Remembrance page (specify who):

- Other social media accounts to be updated/deleted (put a "U" to update/"D" to delete): ____Twitter ____Instagram ____TikTok ____LinkedIn ____Pinterest ____other (specify):

*Make sure to give access to your Executor or a loved one.*

## Location

Location is probably the biggest single factor in determining all of the other details of your memorial service. Location drives many logistical concerns, such as season, indoor or outdoor, theme, number of attendees, and length of time. Cost plays a big role too. You will want to consider your ideal location with care and a few key factors in mind. You also want the location to reflect your personality. Bear in mind your ideal location may not be available in the future, so this will record your key considerations when decisions are to be made.

### *Space*

- Is the location large enough — or intimate enough — to accommodate your event?
- Number of guests preferred (number/range):
- Venue/Room capacity:
- Parking availability: ____yes ____no
- Number of parking spaces:
- ADA accessible: ____yes ____no

- Service pet/Emotional pet (ESA) permitted: ____yes ____no
- Pet friendly (if your "non-service" pet is to be included): ____yes ____no

### *Weather*

- Is the location practical for all seasons?
- Do you have an alternate plan in case of wet, cold, or extremely hot weather?
- What is your alternate plan?

- Is there enough space for an outside tent?

- *VERY IMPORTANT:* If the event is planned for outdoors and you don't want a tent, are there indoor accommodations for an alternate plan?

### *Reservations*

Although you may not be able to preplan a specific date, you can specify the amount of time after death when you would like your Celebration of Life or memorial service held. If you are planning a Living Tribute, reservations are a must.

- How long in advance does the location need to be reserved?

- Do you prefer a specific time of year? ____yes ____no
- When?

- Is there a specific date you prefer for your service?
- Do you have a time of day that you prefer your service be held?

***Specific Venue, if known:***

Name:

Address:

Phone:

***House of Worship, if preferred:***

Name:

Address:

Phone:

***Other Location, if preferred (ex., a park, golf club, restaurant):***

## *Food and Beverage*

Many locations with in-house catering may require you to use their services. This is something to consider when you choose your site. Onsite food and beverage service can be convenient; you will want to ensure the food is good and that minimums dictated align with your guest count. You don't want to end up having money needlessly spent. You can ask for a tasting and/or read reviews online to check the food quality.

If permitted, you can hire an outside caterer and create a list of your own pre-selected menu items. Depending on the type of memorial service, you can also ask friends and family to bring a dish. With any of these choices, an event professional is extremely helpful with organizing the menu and setup, and dealing with location staff.

- Time of Day: ____Breakfast ____Lunch ____Brunch ___Dinner ____Coffee break/snacks ____Cocktail hour ____Heavy hors d'oeuvres ____Full reception
- Sit down or Buffet meal?
- Favorite Catering company:
- Bar: ____yes ____no
- Specialty cocktail: ____yes ____no
- Specialty cocktail name and recipe, especially if your own creation:

- I would like a special toast made in my honor: ___yes ____no
- The person I'd like to give the toast is ________________________________.
- My favorite menu items I'd like to be served:

- I am happy with a potluck gathering at the home of a loved one: ____yes ____no

## Decor and Other Details

Decor can set the tone of your memorial. There are many details that can be considered. This is a list of items to review, primarily for a full-scale event. You may want to glance over these for ideas even if you anticipate a smaller function.

- My favorite color(s):

- I would like them incorporated into my service: ____yes ____no
- Do you have a theme? (ex., favorite hobby, travel destination, artist, book, etc.)

- Design and artwork:

- Signs:

- Staging:

- Backdrop:

- Special lighting:

- Audio/Visual:

- Gobo/projection:

- Specialty furniture:

- High-top cocktail tables:

- Do you have a Graphic Artist who can execute your design preferences?

  ____yes ____no

- Name and contact information of preferred Graphic Artist:

## Readings/Eulogies

Readings and stories personalize a service and communicate your life and legacy. Think about those who know you best, those who can share your story, those you've shared special moments with, and those who can share the very essence of who you are. That's who you want to speak at your service. They do not have to be professional speakers. Family, friends, or colleagues are often the best because they share and speak from the heart.

Conflicts are a part of being human. It is *your* service, so you are free to also state those you do not want to speak.

- Speakers/eulogy:

- Readers:

- Favorite scripture or spiritual passages I'd like read at my service:

- Favorite poems, jokes, or other important words to incorporate:

## Special Services

- Candlelight vigil: ____yes ____no
- Dove release: ____yes ____no
- Butterfly release: ____yes ____no
- Psychic/tarot readings: ____yes ____no
- New Orleans style jazz procession: ____yes ____no
- Other (specify):

- Hearse: ____yes ____no
- Color of hearse: ____black ____white ____other (specify):

- Motorcycle hearse: ____yes ____no
- Carriage: ____yes ____no
- Wagon: ____yes ____no
- Special procession route to be taken (specify):

*Note: While balloons and Chinese lanterns are beautiful sendoffs, many localities are banning their release due to environmental considerations. You may not want either in a green service.*

## Video and Photography

Video and photography are essential to sharing old memories and capturing new ones. Some old photos and audio can be incorporated in a legacy video, as well. *Start recording short videos now.* You can store these on a home computer or flash drive. All the pieces can be edited together to tell your story and presented at your memorial and/or virtually.

- I would like a video documenting my life and legacy: ____yes ____no

- I have video recordings that can be incorporated: ____yes ____no
- Location where my videos are stored:

- If stored in a location needing a password, who has access?

- Favorite photos I would like used in my legacy video are*:

**It would be ideal to label the back of these photos now and store them properly.*

- Location where my photos are stored:

- Songs that represent the soundtrack of my life are*:

**Note: Music use may be subject to copyright laws and fees if viewed in a public setting or online.*

- Videographer:

  Phone:

- Video editor:

  Phone:

- Photographer:

  Phone:

- I'd like my memorial service recorded for my family and friends: ____yes ____no
- Number of guests who may want a copy of my legacy video:

*A skilled event professional/Life Celebrant will be able to help with any of the above items.*

## Notification

How would you like loved ones and guests to be notified about your service? You can assist in the design of a formal invitation if you'd like, where details can be added in at a later date. *There are no rules.*

- Formal invitation: ____yes ____no
- Email invitation: ____yes ____no
- Phone tree: ____yes ____no
- Social media: ____yes ____no
- Dynamic, personalized video invitation with RSVP capability*: ____yes ____no
- Calligraphy for written invites: ____yes ____no
- Color scheme (specify):
- Special theme or design (specify):
- Graphic artist, if known:

Phone:

- I have an updated email contact list: ____yes ____no
- Specify where to find your updated email contact list:

**This is a specialized service. Contact Epilogue Tributes to arrange.*

- Guest book at service: ____yes ____no
- Keepsake for guests (ex., memory book): ____yes ____no
- I would like: ____prayer cards ____bingo cards ____playing cards ____golf cards ____affirmation cards ____angel readings ____other keepsake item (specify):

- Number of guests who may want a copy of my memory book:

## Obituary

Who knows better the details of your life than you? There is absolutely nothing wrong with writing your own obituary. In the growing end-of-life care movement, classes can now be found to help you craft your own. You can also find writers who specialize in this and can work with you, as well.

- Will you be writing your own obituary: ____yes ____no
- Will a loved one write your obituary: ____yes ____no
- Will a professional writer craft your obituary: ____yes ____no

Specify who:

- Where this document will be stored?

## Newspapers or Publications

I would like a death notice or obituary submitted for publication to the following:

- Publication:

- Publication:

- Publication:

- Publication:

- Alumni organization:

- Alumni organization:

- Other organizations:

## Remembrance

Below are some items you may want remembered or reminisced. These are things that brought you the most happiness, or things you consider positive traits that say who you are. Specify if you want them incorporated into your memorial (or obituary).

- My earliest childhood memory:

- What I wanted to be when I grew up:

- Where and how I met my spouse:

- Fondest family memory:

- My first trip:

- Memory of my parent(s):

- A memory with my best friend(s):

- My favorite place:

- My beloved pets:

- Proudest career achievement:

- Favorite hobbies:

- My favorite entertainer(s) and movie:

- Anything else you would like to share?

## Guests and Attendees

In planning ahead, it is beneficial to keep an *updated* list of those you would like to be at your service. Your list should include a current phone number, address, and e-mail for each person noted.

- My up-to-date address book can be found here:

- I have compiled a list of guests/attendees for my service: ____yes ____no
- Location of my guest/attendee list:

To get started:

| NAME | E-MAIL | PHONE | CITY & STATE |
|---|---|---|---|
| | | | |
| | | | |
| | | | |
| | | | |
| | | | |
| | | | |
| | | | |
| | | | |
| | | | |
| | | | |
| | | | |
| | | | |

| NAME | E-MAIL | PHONE | CITY & STATE |
| --- | --- | --- | --- |
| | | | |
| | | | |
| | | | |
| | | | |
| | | | |
| | | | |
| | | | |
| | | | |
| | | | |

## *Travel Considerations*

Arrangements may need to be considered for out-of-town family and guests.

- I expect guests will stay with family or friends: ____yes ____no
- Hotel room(s) or a block may need to be arranged: ____yes ____no
- Hotel and location where a room block can be arranged:

- Breakfast served at this hotel? ____yes ____no
- Nearby restaurants to this hotel? ____yes ____no

- Hotel shuttle/van to transport guests: ____yes ____no
- Other transportation:

- I have designated travel/hotel expenses in the budget for out of town guests: ____yes ____no

## My Legacy Lives On

I firmly believe everyone has come here with a unique gift and purpose. In addition to your personalized memorial service, is there anything your family can do "to pay it forward" as a remembrance of you that will live on? For example: donating your books and creating a library in your memory, raising money annually for your favorite cause, starting a scholarship, or creating a nonprofit. Specify if there is a legacy project you would like to see come to fruition to honor your life:

## *"Love Burns Across the Infinitude."*

The Universe is made up completely of energy. This includes humans. I want you to take some time and consider that we return to this universal energy when we die. Our body may be gone, but our spirit energy remains. Many of those left behind take comfort in signs from loved ones from beyond. What sign or symbol will you use to communicate with those you leave behind? Make it as personal, unique and/or complicated as you want and note it here:

I ______________________________________ have thoroughly and thoughtfully prepared these details with my loved ones in mind. I want my family and friends to celebrate me and remember me with lasting memories and love in their hearts.

______________________________________

**Signature**

______________________________________

**Print Name**

I have shared my plan with the following whom I entrust to carry out this plan:

___________________________________________________

**Executor Name**

___________________________________________________

**Designated Agent**

___________________________________________________

**Trusted Family or Friend**

*Please remember to inform the above where to find this Planner.*

## Author Bio

Felicia Barlow Clar is a Sacred Life Celebrant, award-winning producer and writer. She has produced hundreds of corporate and private events, festivals, and award winning videos. For more than 25 years, she has explored deeply spirituality, metaphysics, transformation and self awareness work.

Felicia combined these two facets of her life when, in less than a year and half, she lost both her beloved stepfather and sister. Wanting to celebrate them and their unique contributions, she was able to bring her event expertise to the funeral home process and personalize their memorials, which included dancing at the end of her sister's service. She transformed the experience from suffering to gratitude and joy.

She is the creator of Epilogue Tributes, a niche event company supporting the bereaved with memorial planning and celebrations of life, workbooks, and consulting on end-of-life options. She has received end-of-life CareDoula® education from Quality of Life Care. She has been published in *Elephant Journal,* and her production credits include NBC, HBO, E!, Food Network, Discovery, and PBS.

www.ingramcontent.com/pod-product-compliance
Lightning Source LLC
LaVergne TN
LVHW061257100826
845148LV00008B/1158

* 9 7 8 1 7 3 6 8 2 5 1 2 9 *